Maybe You're Dead

Caroline Axe

BookLeaf
Publishing

Presentation by *BookLeaf Publishing*

Web: www.bookleafpub.com

E-mail: info@bookleafpub.com

ISBN: 978-93-95784-54-2

First edition 2022

DEDICATION

This book is dedicated to my Uncle David who had a passion for stories and above all writing.

PREFACE

Verses and scribbled pen on bits of paper, books and note pads i found.

Strange

Tumble weeds are blowing
Slight breeze is flowing

Along the horizon of my mind
The closing of the blinds and the change
Of passing time

Takes me away
Away with the chimes of enticing rain
Washing away the pain of strange

Blank

Blank Blank Blank
Emptiness confides in me
Along the road to
Loneliness
Unfolds a new way
A different image
Talking to me deep inside

Breakout

Nothing colour
Bland whiteness
The thickness
Suffocating
The madness of it all
Trapped by the brightness
Breaking free, shouting out
Shimmers of colours
Through the colours of my mind
Shaking my head to try and find

Something else

Star

Stars falling down

Crashing making a mess

I see the colour drained

From their eye

This is their heaven, not in the sky

Look up, not away

The're trying to say.

Greed

5

Greed
I want more
Your sunshine ora
Kills my night
With sparkling eyes you are like
The air that I breath, keeping me
Alive
Spirit
I like it like this

Clockface

Clockface numbers entwined
The days push past in a hurry and the night is
bold
Keep your eyes tightly shut
The fear of waking is too much

How long can you hold on
The deep blackness
That swallows you whole
All this behind the blinds

As daylight slowly climbs
The only thing that keeps me sane
Is knowing the sun
Will come up again

Looking at the clockface

What is love

What is love?
Excitement
a constant buzz
continuous and rushing.
It's not a word
but a whole feeling you can't explain
Insane
with happiness
An original trance

Does love

Does love flower and bloom
Has love a colour so true and bold

Does love wilt like a rose, it's glow fading
through coldness

Is love a spirit, the quietness of its voice you
cannot hear.
Making up it's own mind
Spinning around and around up to the sun
Giving warmth to free us all

Addict

I love you in my mind
My love accumulates all the time.
I'm an addict to your deception
you have the control now take the power.

But you are dazed when I sit up and as I
decipher your thoughts
our body language begins to talk
My great debut, with you
My luck, my way
Iluminous lust and love, of course
Denial
Chemistry is there, I've seen it spark
We are flammable

Truelove

When sweet lips do touch
Is it lust

When love flowers
Is it haste
Or does your heart warm to mine

Don't hold in vain, this mutual fear of its glow
fading.

Close to you

Starting up,
we're together
But coldness keeps us apart.
I'm afraid
for me
wanting
You
Forever
There are waves that keep us close but far apart.
Pure tears of kindness
Crying out for you
Please don't leave me
I won't let you go

Invisible

Space,
Between us
Courteous but curious
Illusional love
Invisible love
Magnetic
Cloudy visions, its hard to see the doors which
are locked.
Your emotions are the keys,
Please
Listen to me
Fly

Dreams

Sounds, mixed up in your head
floating around.
Spinning like bubbles
freedom, emotions flow
You're lost in another frequency
Let yourself go
Lock away everything, for a while.
Stop, the end
This is the end.
Your bubble bursts your dreams
But dreams are ambitions and ambitions become
reality
Combing across your mind

Entwined

The phases we go through
Our minds twist and turn
The need of wanting violently churns
You are the victim
Of a circle of love
Your soul is aching
Searching through clouds of time
The gold is glistening but its hard to find
Reaching, touching the bronze as it turns to
silver dust.
Through your touch and mine

Void

I have lots on my mind
But nothing to say
The jigsaw is broken,
But a blur in our eyes
Sunshine follows on our false display
Always the depth of the darkness
Plunges into our world
Private

Goodbye

All the time I've given you
Sick of all the memories, it's all true

With the designs in my eye
Like the cemetery gates shutting
It's time to say goodbye

That love that dims a low light in me
How can it burn

That love that shines so bright in me
When will it return

Friends

Running through the streets we laughed
not a care, the sound of friendship all around,
the sun beating down
we share this moment, it will not last.
But the happiness in our hearts will keep us
going.
The friends we have when we were younger
Enable us to live longer
On the promise that this feeling will return
Your friends when you were younger.

Days

Wake up
Lazy days
Dead days
Forgotten days
Days gone by
Days to come
Horizon days
Look beyond days
What the future holds days
Better days
Don't get stuck in sinking sand

Safety

Smells, warmth, homely
Soft, sleepy
Blend.
Plunge deep into the atmosphere created
Wrapping my arms around
Swirling around and around
Calm
Collected
Solid

Tomorrow

Tomorrow is today and yesterday has gone.
A smile a laugh
Time flickers past
Grab your chance and make it last.
Spinning around you fall to the ground.
Viewers from the outside
Alone in the dark.

Later

The kindness of your smile
Wanting to converse
Your mind bursting at the seems as the words
fall onto paper
But it can wait till later

The constant ticking of the clock
The slow dripping from the tap
The stars are out there, they provide the map
A piece of film that warms your heart
A news story you've followed from the start
But it can wait till later

Chats with biscuits and freshly brewed tea
The days expectations for all to see
Ideas are the leaves that have fallen from the tree
All alone and just be
But it can wait till later

You should be here
We are all surrounded by the fear
Of not letting anyone near and now you should
be the one here
It can't wait till later